SOUTH EASTERN SAIL

From the Medway to the Solent 1840 - 1940

Topsail schooner at Sandwich, 1861

SOUTH EASTERN SAIL

From the Medway to the Solent 1840 - 1940

Michael Bouquet

David & Charles : Newton Abbot

FOR MARY BOUQUET AND MARGARET MICHELL,
Granddaughters of Captain Matthew Michell
of the schooner *Bertha*, with love

ISBN 0 7153 5592 9

Set in 11 on 13 point Baskerville
and printed in Great Britain
by W. J. Holman Limited Dawlish
for David & Charles (Publishers) Limited
South Devon House Newton Abbot Devon

Contents

This book is a deliberate exercise in recall of a marine landscape that few living eyes have seen nor living memory experienced. Though my period extends from 1840 to 1940, this book is in essence about the sailing ships and ports of south-eastern England between 1850 and 1900. Unlike the havens described in my *Westcountry Sail*, where sail-using ships lingered on until 1950, in south-eastern England most wooden shipbuilding had finished by 1880; most local deep-water ships had sailed for the last time by 1890; by 1914 most locally owned sailing coasters had gone. The sailing barges of Swale and Medway struggled on until after World War II. Rye and Littlehampton built a few wooden coasters. But the great days of sail in the South East are now beyond living memory.

True, in the 1930s there were still sail-using craft in the South East—barges, Dutch auxiliary coasters like the *Margina* (below), built at Groningen in 1920. Westcountry vessels and Baltic timber ships like the *Alastor* (pages 74-81). Up to 1939 one could see from Beachy Head or the South Foreland the Finnish grain ships or the German nitrate ships bound for

The Dutch schooner *Margina* and the cross-Channel ferry *Prince Leopold* in the Dover Straits, 1936.

The Eastbourne lifeboat puts off to the *Davenport*, 27 February 1936.

the London River or Hamburg. But these were not craft native to the region; no one could call South East England a haunt of sailing ships.

Nevertheless in the 1930s there were still plenty of people alive whose memories went back to the years of sail. There were many more who had heard at first hand from an older generation of the great days of the mid-nineteenth century. At Faversham there was Captain Waters, twenty-seven years master of the *Goldfinch*. At Newhaven there was Captain J. Robinson, a retired pilot who had commanded the brigantines *Amanda* and *Sussex Maid* (pages 51 and 47) and who knew so much about the sailing ships of the Ouse.

At Shoreham there were men who had sailed in Penney's emigrant ships (pages 65-81); others who had served in the Black Sea grain trade or who remembered running down their easting in little 400 ton barques from Mauritius to Australia. There was Henry Cheal at the Marlipins Museum whose *Ships and Mariners of Shoreham* (1909) had tapped the memories of an even earlier generation. There was John McCoy born in 1860, who ran away to sea in a Jersey potato smack at the age of ten, had served his time in the brig *Sarah* and sailed in the Mauritius trade in the 327 ton *Eurus* in the eighties (page 60-1).

At Littlehampton, Hilder Harvey of the local shipbuilding firm was still alive with memories of a voyage to the Falkland Islands in the Littlehampton barque *Trossachs*. Miss Ginner at Hastings remembered the loss of her father's collier *Pelican* in 1879 (pages 35-9). Old fishermen at Eastbourne could point out where the brig *Bee* had discharged coal on the beach. These were the memories of the old people; memories of the sailing colliers, the North Sea traders and above all of what they called the colonial trade to New Zealand, Australia, South Africa and the Mauritius, (always with the definite article).

In these pages I have tried to illustrate and to comment upon the memories and the myths of those old friends of mine. I have not in general referred to the spritsail barges of the Thames and the Medway; theirs is a specialist study. Nor have I set out to discuss fishing boats or naval craft. Instead I have concentrated on those trading vessels which operated in a region dominated by the metropolis.

Hence the early nineteenth-century packet services, the hoys of North Kent and the barges working up the Thames with straw, hay or corn for London's horses. The resorts which burgeoned with the arrival of the railways needed house and gas coal, building materials and provisions, much of which came by sea for many decades. Coal from the North East gave a living to scores of brigs and schooners built of Wealden oak in Sussex shipyards. Such colliers entered every port between Portsmouth and Rochester. The same vessels could make the occasional voyage across the North Sea for Scandinavian timber. The repeal of the Corn Laws opened up the Black Sea grain trade to British barques and brigs. Rye and Hastings specialised in fast schooners for the Azores orange trade while Shoreham and Newhaven were building superb small square-riggers for oceanic trade. Some of these later became colliers sailing out of Whitstable, Dover, Newhaven or Portsmouth. Up to the second decade of this century shallow-draught wooden ketch barges were still being built in the region. In the eighties Southampton was launching classic steel Cape Horners.

The ports of Kent, Sussex and Hampshire face out to one of the busiest sea-lanes in the northern hemisphere. The ships of 1850 to 1890 were more numerous, individually smaller and more vulnerable to disaster than modern cargo ships. The shipwreck pages reveal that the sailing ship large or small was all too often a dangerous mode of transport. No wonder that these coasts have seen their share of marine casualties. Collisions and founderings were usual happenings. It is unfortunate, but true, that some of the older wooden sailing ships were notoriously unseaworthy. Plimsoll's 'Black List' of ships due for survey, which he handed to the Board of Trade in June 1873, contained the names of five Sussex colliers. In 1872 when a principal surveyor of the Board of Trade described the brig *Circassian* of Shoreham as 'dangerously unsafe and altogether unseaworthy', the owner's agent called out 'Damn your eyes!' and abused the unfortunate surveyor in the street. Some ships were horrific; mere floating death-traps for their wretched crews. Beware of a too romantic image of the sailing ship!

I can remember when the ketch barge *Davenport* was wrecked at Eastbourne in February 1936 (p7). She was an interesting vessel rigged with the half-sprit of the seventeenth century, and must have been the last sailing vessel wrecked on our south-eastern coast.

Though I have had access to many more pictures than I could possibly use it has been harder to provide a variety of illustrative material, and it has been very hard indeed to find photographs of life on board south-eastern sailing ships. Sail in south-eastern England was at its height in the period 1850-1900, when photography was still relatively expensive and difficult. All honour to those pioneer photographers who were portraying ships in the nineteenth century. Their names deserve recording and in my list of sources of illustrations I have tried to do this in the rare cases where the nineteenth-century photographer's name is known.

I began collecting these pictures in 1931 while I was still at school; the latest came in this year. Forty years is a long time to hang around. Let us be under way among the vanished ships and in the crowded havens of a by-gone age, under the white cliffs where 'the sheep-bells and the ship-bells ring'.

Kent — The North and East Coast

Kent is one of the three English counties with a north and a south coast. This lengthy shore-line from Dartford to Dungeness is the home of ancient havens, busy ports and navigable creeks; all of which were thronged with shipping in the days of sail. The Kentish shore properly begins at Greenhithe, once the home of the Everard sailing barges, but out of the Thames estuary and the port of London the first real Kentish port is Rochester on the Medway. With its hinterland of rich Kentish countryside, Rochester was a shipowning town far back in the past. In the mid-nineteenth century Rochester ships were owned by farmers, brewers, brickmakers, shipbuilders, corn factors, confectioners and sailmakers. In 1865 there were 196 sailing vessels owned in the port. Of these 120 were barges, the common carriers of the Thames and Medway. The rest were brigs and schooners with a barque or two. In 1865 Rochester's largest vessel was the barque *Isabella Harnett*, 405 tons, built in 1844.

Below is a typical scene within the port of Rochester in the late 1920s. Limehouse Reach in the Medway with St Mary's, Chatham in the background, and the Cornish schooner *Trevellas* is discharging china clay into a lighter. She was lost with all hands in 1930. Two Medway sailing barges are moored waiting, like so many barges at that time, for the cargoes that never came . . .

Faversham, on a creek off the Swale, has long been a shipbuilding and shipowning port. In 1865 there were 207 Faversham-registered vessels owned in Faversham, Sittingbourne and Whitstable, a few even in Canterbury. Only twenty-nine were barges, the rest were brigs, brigantines and schooners.

The port's most interesting vessel was the schooner barge *Goldfinch* (above), built by J. M. Goldfinch in 1894. She had the flat-bottomed hull and leeboards of the barge, with the conventional rig of the topsail schooner, later modified to a ketch rig with square topsails. After sailing out of Faversham for thirty-six years, the *Goldfinch* was sold in 1930 to owners in British Guiana, crossing the Atlantic in forty-five days. She carried cargoes on the Berbice River until 1947 when she was condemned.

The great occupation of Whitstable ships (top opposite) was the coal trade from the north of England. In the earlier part of our period Whitstable ships had a bad name as maritime disgraces, ending their long careers by pumping their way up and down the East coast. Life for the crews aboard them was grim. But towards the end of the century many of the smaller shipowners of north Kent amalgamated under the management of the Whitstable Shipping Co and a better type of ship, though still likely to be elderly, sailed out of the harbour. Here are three Faversham-registered brigantines in Whitstable towards the turn of the century. From left to right they are the *Joseph* (built 1879), the *Carmenta* (1875) and the *L. C. Owen* (1868). All three were built in Prince Edward Island.

Local coasters sailed out of creeks like Halstow, Milton, Sittingbourne or Conyer. A few discharged their cargoes on open beaches, as in this photograph taken at Herne Bay towards the close of the century. A small schooner believed to be the *Bee* has been run on the beach at the top of high water to discharge her cargo over the side. The patient horses wait in the water and the holiday children play on the shingle.

'Can I forget thee, old Margate hoy?' wrote Charles Lamb in an agreeable essay, nostalgic for the vessels which once carried London's holiday-makers. Clark Russell wrote more realistically, 'No! You want to live a long way from a vessel of this kind to find any sort of romance in her navigations'. Indeed, to watch the hoys come in from London was to gloat over the misery of their wretched passengers as they staggered ashore.

'Why as fast as the boats fill, the deck is covered again with new faces that rise out of the hold. There is no end of it.— I will positively count no more—Nay ladies, you need not say how sick you have been,—your looks will vouch for you.—A tedious passage,—a high sea,— all the pumps continually going,—and no room to stir, even to the ship's side on necessary calls—it is monstrously inconvenient!—but it is a *party of pleasure, and that is enough.*' (Keate, *Sketches from Nature,* 1802.)

A year or two after Waterloo the first excursion steamers were running on the Thames and within a decade the hoys had gone. Many Margate hoys were built at Broadstairs where White was the shipbuilder. In 1795 he built the hoy *Princess of Wales,* 75 tons. She sailed from London on Saturdays and returned from Margate on Tuesdays. Sometimes she continued from Margate to Ostend and called again at Margate on the return trip. In 1820 the *Princess of Wales* was bought for a sealing voyage to the South Indian Ocean. In a heavy swell and a dead calm she was driven ashore in the Crozets. Her crew had the most extraordinary adventures before reaching civilization. The voyage of this Margate hoy is described in Charles Goodridge's *Narrative of a Voyage to the South Seas* published at Exeter in 1839. (Below) A Margate hoy and an excursion steamer.

Ramsgate began as a small fishing village overshadowed by Sandwich. It was of little importance until Smeaton gave it its fine harbour (1780-95), followed by the lighthouse soon after. These were paid for in part by 'The Royal Harbour of Ramsgate Duty' levied on passing shipping (above). But high harbour dues rendered the magnificent harbour unattractive to mid-nineteenth century shipping. Often there was little inside those superb piers except for fishing boats. In 1865 Ramsgate and Margate between them owned only thirty-one sailing ships. There was little trade apart from imports of coal and timber for local use.

Ramsgate's importance was as a useful service station. The receipt above emphasises the presence of the Harbour Trustees' steam tug *Samson*. Not only could a tug assist distressed vessels into the harbour, it could also tow a pulling and sailing lifeboat out to a vessel on the Goodwins or the Sunk. 'These tugs necessarily enable Ramsgate to achieve a very great deal more in the way of lifesaving than Deal or Broadstairs. At best the lifeboat sails poorly, 'ratches' clumsily and sluggishly, and there is nothing to be done with her in the face of a dead inshore wind. Again and again Broadstairs and Deal have had to look idly on while the Ramsgate tug has been towing the lifeboat of the place to a spot where a ship is going to pieces.' When Clark Russell wrote this in 1889 he estimated that from 1865 to 1889 Ramsgate boatmen had saved 850 lives (next pages).

A tug towing a lifeboat to windward of a wreck

Nearly noon at Ramsgate in mid-century (top right). Longshoremen and harbour officials gossip round the warping capstan and bollards near the old dry dock—filled in in about 1893. In the dry dock is a magnificent wooden full-rigger of about 600 tons, a reminder of that period when 1000 tons represented a very big ship indeed. The Clock House, built about 1819, was reroofed and had its stonework cleaned in 1971.

Early this century the paddle tug *Aid,* built in 1899, tows a Danish timber barquentine out of Ramsgate. She is a heavily sparred vessel with a fore royal. A local fishing smack is on the other side of the tug, and a Thames barge is astern of the barquentine.

Sandwich (vignette p 1) has long been of minor maritime importance. Once a Cinque port and once the port of Canterbury, by 1850 only a few small coasters, like the schooner in the engraving, found their way through the mud of Pegwell Bay and up the Stour. In 1909 the famous schooner *Result* of Barnstaple, now preserved by the Ulster Folk Museum, was one of the last sailing coasters to visit the quay below the bridge. In 1850 a schooner the *Mystery* was built here.

The windbound
fleet leaves the
Downs

Conrad wrote of hearing 'upwards of ten score of windlasses spring like one into clanking life in the dead of night, filling the Downs with a panic-struck sound of anchors being torn hurriedly out of the ground at the approach of an easterly wind'.

It was a noble sight in the great anchorage of the Downs abreast of Deal, after a long spell of sou'westerly winds, when perhaps two or three hundred sailing vessels all outward bound had accumulated in the anchorage. As soon as the wind shifted to the eastward, the great fleet used to get under way together, all with one object—to get to the westward and out of the Channel as soon as possible.

Equally impressive was the scene after a spell of March easterly winds, when the wind had shifted to the westward and hundreds of ships of the windbound fleet hove-up, ran out their studdingsail booms and set every rag of canvas. In Edwin Weedon's spirited engraving ships large and small are racing home. In the midst of them all is a tiny Deal lugger. Perhaps two or three of her crew are aboard different ships accompanying them to their destinations. No men in the world were more ready to face danger than the Deal boatmen.

16

The lugger in the left-hand picture has her mainsail set, but in this picture the luggers are out in heavy weather and their mainmasts are unstepped. This engraving, called *A Deal lugger making for a ship on the Goodwins*, which appeared in the *Illustrated London News* in October 1872, was the last which Weedon executed for that periodical before his death. The *raison d'etre* for these big luggers—up to 20 tons and 34ft long—was to assist ships in bad weather, particularly those on the Goodwins. When the Downs were full of sailing ships the Goodwins, extending nine to ten miles from north to south, were a protective break-water. But they were extremely dangerous to sailing ships outside in an easterly gale, and in certain states of the wind even to those entering the roadstead. If a vessel got entangled in the sands in daylight, or if rocket signals were seen at night, the Deal 'hovellers' would launch their luggers from the open beach and be on their way to help.

Clark Russell described the Deal lugger as 'a noble boat; a wonderful structure to en-counter Channel weather in; the most weatherly of marine structures'. From 1860 to 1887 fifty-three lugger men were drowned at their work: a sufficient answer to those who alleged that the Deal 'hovellers' earned rich pickings from the misfortunes of others. The luggers were an essential part of the maritime scene at this corner of south-east England.

Dover likes to describe itself as 'The Gateway of England', and it has, of course, been pre-eminent for its cross-Channel services since Tudor times. But as the only deep-water port between London and Southampton it has always handled a great volume of maritime traffic apart from the ferry business. Here at the turn of the century the harbour tug *Lady Crundall* is edging an unnamed Norwegian barque into the Granville Dock. This wooden sailing ship with a rail around her poop is interesting because she has a standing gaff on the mizzen with the spanker brailed into the mast. The elaborate carved and painted ornament on the stern and quarter is a real piece of folk art. This picture is by the Dover photographers Amos & Amos, whose original glass negatives, now at Greenwich, are an invaluable record of sailing vessels in or off Dover at the beginning of the century.

This view of Folkestone harbour in about 1880 shows a rare array of local sailing colliers; it reminds us that the port had a maritime life quite distinct from its busy cross-Channel traffic. Left to right are the Seamen's Mission ketch; the brigantine *Edna*, built in Prince Edward Island in 1871; the brig *William & Antony*, built at Charlestown, Cornwall, in 1862; the brigantine *Enterprise*, probably the one of that name built at Prince Edward Island in 1860; and a second *Edna*, built on the island in 1877. There are several vessels no longer identifiable and at the end of the line is the snow *Cambois*, built at Blyth in 1870. The preponderance of Prince Edward Island-built vessels in this picture and that of Whitstable (p 11) illustrates how popular these ships were among British shipowners. They were cheap to build, they were constructed to almost standardised designs, and it has even been suggested that there was a degree of built-in obsolescence about them. It paid owners engaged in businesses like the coal trade to buy an island-built vessel cheaply, and scrap or sell it after a comparatively short working life; rather than to tie up capital in a more long lived ship which might cost twice as much.

The original Five Ports—as they were described until the sixteenth century—did not include Rye. Rye and Winchelsea, originally attached as members of Hastings, obtained equal membership in the fourteenth century as 'antient towns'. At its greatest extent the confederation consisted of forty-two towns, the great majority of which now answer to Kipling's description—'ports of stranded pride'.

But at the beginning of the nineteenth century Rye still survived as a port with an agricultural hinterland. Much of its sea-borne commerce was doubtless at the level of the vessels named in this sailing card—small packet ships sailing for the Thames with local produce and returning with goods for Rye and the surrounding Romney Marsh villages. The *Friends of Liberty* was a sloop of 40 tons, built at Rye in 1813; the *Nancy*, a similar sloop, was built in 1811.

Some Rye ships crossed the Atlantic. The brig *William*, 108 tons, whose master was Samuel Vidler, was built at Rye in 1815. She crossed from there to New York in seventy-one days in 1830 with emigrants. In 1832 she was advertised to sail from Rye to St John, N.B. The *William* was lost near Holy Island in December 1851.

NOW LOADING AT

Griffin's Wharf, Southwark,

For RYE,

Robins and Sons,
Printers, Tooley-Street

FRIENDS OF LIBERTY ....William Rogers.
AMITY .... Edward Fowle.
NANCY ....George French

The *Nancy* *French*, **Master.**

Takes in Goods for

Appledore	Ewhurst	Pert	Selscomb	Wittersham
Beckley	Lydd	Rolvenden	Staple-Cross	Woodchurch
Breede	Northiam	Robertsbridge	Tenderden	and all places
Brookland	Newenden	Romney	Uddimore	adjacent.
Benenden	Peasemarsh	Sandhurst	Winchelsea	

₊ Goods for the above places are not received at this Wharf but on the conditions following, to say, that the Proprietors will not be accountable, or engage to forward them by any particular vessel named in the receipt given, neither loss by fire, vermin, high tides, leakage or wastage, act of God, king's enemies, or loss occasioned by imperfect directions, marks or packing. Neither will any advice be given of the shipment of goods which may be left out of former vessels. The act of God, the king's enemies, fire, and all and every the dangers and accidents of the seas, rivers, and navigation, of whatever nature or kind soever, excepted.
The Captain or Wharfingers to be spoke with on the Irish Walk in 'Change hours.

The last day of taking in goods is
1833

Received for **Thomas Farncomb**, Wharfinger.

84 Packages ....
Articles 14/

11/3

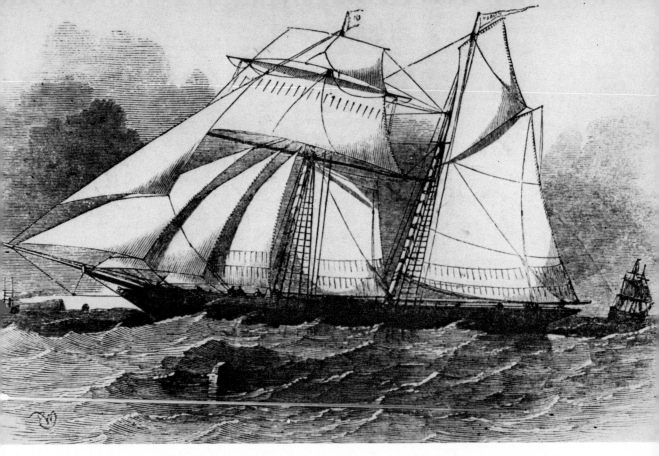

In the middle of the century, Rye shared in the general shipping boom. In 1865 fifty-six merchant ships were owned in the port including several from Hastings. As a shipbuilding centre the town was well known and busy. The shipbuilders were Hoad Brothers and Hessell & Holmes. A visitor to Rye in 1855 wrote home to Devon that Rye 'is not so large as Newton Abbot, and there does not seem to be doing much except shipbuilding. There is seven ships building from 200 to 300 tons.'

One of the more publicised Rye ships was the *Marion Zagury*, 98 tons, launched on 12 January 1853 by Hessell & Holmes for Samuel Zagury of London for the African and Mediterranean trades. The *Illustrated London News* woodcut, after a sketch by Weedon, shows her as a typical heavily canvassed fruit schooner; the master, four men and a boy would take a ship like this anywhere in the North Atlantic. It was not unknown for a vessel of this type to force a passage to windward against a south-westerly gale, pass through a big fleet of wind-bound ships in the Downs, go out to the Azores, load a cargo of oranges and to be back in the Downs within three weeks to find the same ships still delayed there.

Britons never shall be Slaves.

RYE RYE

SHIPWRIGHTS V. SHIPWRIGHTS.

A GRAND MATCH OF
Cricket

WILL BE PLAYED ON THE

TOWN SALTS, RYE,

on MONDAY, JULY 16th, 1849,

BETWEEN ELEVEN SHIPWRIGHTS OF

Messrs. Hoad Brothers,

AND ELEVEN SHIPWRIGHTS OF

MESSRS. HESSELL AND HOLMES,

FOR TEN SOVEREIGNS.

WICKETS TO BE PITCHED AT ONE O'CLOCK.

A GOOD SUPPER will be provided, at the HOPE & ANCHOR
INN, for the players, in the evening, and for any friend who
may be pleased to honour them with their company,
by the puplic's obedient servant.
EDWARD FOWLE.

H. P. Clark, Printer, Rye.

Rye shipwrights relaxed in friendly rivalry with a game of cricket. On working days the competition between the two yards was intense, and it was common for each to launch a vessel on the same tide. This happened for instance in June 1851 when Hessell & Holmes launched the schooner *Anderida* for the fruit trade, and Hoad Bros launched the brig *Effort* for the South American trade. In May 1853 the brigs *Lord Dacre* (Hoad Brothers) and *Topsy* (Hessell & Holmes) were launched on the same tide.

Both firms owned ships as well as building them. Hessell & Holmes built and owned the schooner *Sky Rocket* (1850). Hoad Brothers built and owned the schooner *Impetuous* (1855).

A minor shipbuilding firm was Mills & Son who launched the schooner *Cautious* in 1854.

'She's going down to Rye to make a keel for a Lowestoft fishin' boat,' one of the characters in Kipling's *Rewards and Fairies* says of a great stick of Wealden timber. That particular stick would have gone to the shipbuilding yard of G & T Smith. At the turn of the century the Smiths were building ketch barges as well as trawlers for Lowestoft and Yarmouth owners. This group of workmen at the Smiths' yard about 1895 hold the tools of their craft—maul, adze and saw.

Behind the group is a planked up trawler and another partially in frame. The old men in the party would be of an age to remember the Grand Match of Cricket of half a century before.

As well as the trawlers the Smiths built several ketch barges for the general coasting trade. Commonly known as 'boomies' they had the gaff and boom of the ketch as opposed to the sprit of the Thames barge. Shallow-draughted and flat-bottomed they had the barges' leeboards to enable them to go to windward. One of Smiths' ketch barges was the *Martinet* of Goole (next page), 120 tons, launched in 1912. She survived under sail until 1941, the last of the boomie barges. A German plane dropped seven bombs near her off the NE Gunfleet and she foundered the next morning in Hollesley Bay near Aldeburgh, too badly shaken to hold out until help could get to her.

When I took this photograph of the *Martinet*, her skipper was Bob Roberts, until last year at sea as owner and master of the sailing barge *Cambria*. He wrote to me about the *Martinet*, 'She was a nice old barge, fast off the wind, good in a sea and comfortable to live aboard. She was my home for over two years'. A lovely epitaph for a ship.

Between the wars, Rye's Town Quay and Rye harbour, further down the river were visited by many small coasters with auxiliary engines. Here is the *Hilda* of Delfzijl, 110 tons, steel-built in Zoutkamp in 1910 as the sailing vessel *Anke*. The *Hilda* represents the transition period in the Netherlands' coasting fleet. Originally a two-masted schooner, she still sets two headsails and a trysail, and carries leeboards. The *roef*, or deckhouse, is still much in evidence, but a wheelhouse has been added aft. In the next generation of fully-powered coasters the *roef* and wheelhouse would be combined in a single structure aft, and the last vestiges of canvas would have vanished. When this photograph was taken at Rye harbour in 1935, the new Dutch coasters were already fully-powered.

In the picture below (opposite) taken at the Strand about 1935, two interesting craft have come up the Rother. On the right is the Dutch *Twin* of Kielwindeweer, built in 1932. A fully-powered motorship, the *Twin* has a vestigial link with the past in a trysail.

Ahead of the *Twin* is the wooden spreety barge *Olive May*, 160 tons, built at Sittingbourne in 1920 and the last sail-using vessel to be owned in Rye. She has had a motor installed, which has involved the removal of her mizzen and the building of a wheelhouse.

Chicago, which a quarter of a century before had been a mere trading post in the wilderness, was by 1857 a city of 60,000—the metropolis of the far west. In the early morning of 14 July a tiny ship sailed across the waters of Lake Michigan to berth at the north pier. Within hours a crowd had assembled; by noon a city alderman was making an address of welcome to the master. The next day the story made headlines in the local press—the first ship direct from Europe had arrived!

This vessel was one of Hessell & Holmes' schooners, the *Madeira Pet*, 83 tons, launched at Rye in November 1850 by Don Miguel, Pretender to the Portuguese throne. She was 97ft long with an 18ft beam. She was built for the Azores orange trade. In 1857 she was owned by G. F. Carrington, a Guernsey sailmaker and one of that island's leading shipowners. Soon after her arrival, the *Madeira Pet* was towed to her discharging berth at the foot of La Salle Street. A crowd of several hundreds awaited her arrival. '"Three cheers for the *Madeira Pet*!" rent the air, and her decks were soon covered by the multitude who were anxious to

THE CHICAGO PRESS

OFFICIAL PAPER OF THE CITY.

WEDNESDAY MORNING, JULY 15, 1857.

An Infamous Perversion.

The Washington *Union* of the 11th instant, in a leader entitled "The Question Settled," gives expression to the following atrocious falsehood:

The Kansas troubles are a mere prolongation of the Missouri controversy, in which the abolitionists of every hue in every part of the Northern States insist upon forcing another new State to adopt a Constitution which it does not prefer.

The "Missouri controversy" was settled by the adoption of the Missouri Compromise—that instrument of which Mr. Douglas in his better days declared, that its origin was akin to that of the federal Constitution itself—and the "Kansas

Direct Trade with Europe Accomplished.

ARRIVAL OF THE SCHR. MADEIRA PET FROM LIVERPOOL.

Action of the Chicago Board of Trade.

Yesterday morning the British schooner Madeira Pet, from Liverpool direct, dropped into our river, and modestly lay-to at the north pier, near the mouth of the harbor. Intelligence of the arrival, however, soon reached the city, and before 10 o'clock she was visited by large numbers of our citizens, who were anxious to look upon the first British vessel that had made the passage from Liverpool to Chicago. The question of Direct Trade with Europe had, it is true, already been satisfactorily demonstrated by the trip last year of the barque Dean Richmond, from this port to Liverpool; but that was looked upon by many as merely the American side of the argument. The solution of the problem in

to Messrs. I. H. Burch & Co., of this city. Mr. T. R. Gordon, of New York, now here, is agent of the consignees.

We suggest to our merchants the importance of rewarding this enterprise, by promptly coming forward and purchasing the goods brought to our docks by the Madeira Pet, and thus showing the parties interested that *direct trade* is worth repeating.

We may here state that another cargo is on the way up, which had to be transhipped into the schooner Young America. She will be here in a few days. The same parties are the originators and consignees.

The Madeira Pet is chartered for the round voyage, and will take a return cargo of wheat, corn, or some other product of the Northwest.

Further particulars of the passage of the Madeira Pet will be found in the Marine column on the first page.

Editor's Table.

DIRECT TRADE OF CHICAGO WITH EUROPE.—The all-engrossing topic, in monetary and commercial circles, for the day, is the influence, prospective, on the fortunes of our city, likely to be exerted by the direct trade with foreign marts which has within the past season grown from a vague dream into a defined reality. The Madeira Pet has, by her appearance in our harbor, settled the matter, that our neighbors across the water, alive to the importance of the subject, have seized the first opportunity to reciprocate, "by a return of the compliment," the enterprise of our own merchants, in proffering to them the offer of an interchange of fraternal and commercial intercourse direct, without the aid of our seaboard cities.

around Europe; we know that a ship has sailed from the West of Europe to the State of Illinois—our own Prairie State. Though we are not, we are sorry to say, witty—not even funny—we claim to be very good natured, and on this occasion acknowledge feeling kindly to all the world, but pre-eminently so to Capt. Crang, the commander of the little British vessel that has just now sailed into Chicago harbor. Hearing of our commercial importance—present and prospective—he is the first of our cousins over the water who determined to show, by occular demonstration, that "some things can be done as well as others"—in short, that a direct communication can be profitably opened between the port of Liverpool and that of Chicago.

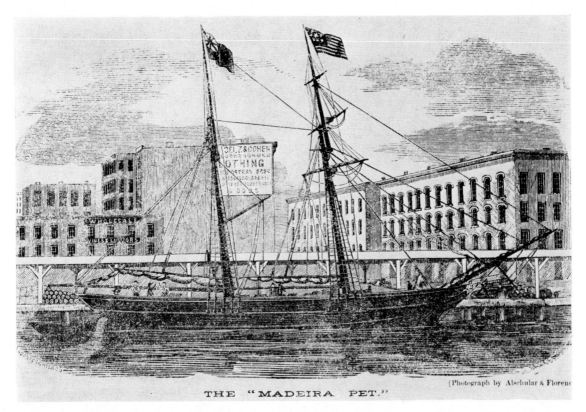

THE "MADEIRA PET."

set foot on the first vessel that had sailed direct from Europe to this port.' (*Chicago Daily Press*, 15 July 1857.)

On the fifteenth, more excitement. Hundreds of sightseers visited the schooner. The Chicago Light Artillery fired a salute of 100 guns; the Great Western Band played *God Save the Queen* and *Yankee Doodle*; at midnight Leland's Light Guard Band ended a busy day with 'a most beautiful serenade.'

Not until the sixteenth did the discharge of her cargo begin—240 tons of cutlery, earthenware, paints, glassware and china from Liverpool. She loaded back for the Mersey with 4,000 cured hides and a barrel of whitefish for Queen Victoria. When she towed out to Lake Michigan on 5 August she was accompanied by merchants, members of the Board of Trade, city councillors and the ubiquitous Light Guard Band.

This little Rye schooner was something altogether new on the Great Lakes. When she left the Detroit River on her inward passage the *Madeira Pet* was in company with thirty sail of Lake vessels—beautiful schooners with centreboards and triangular raffee topsails. She managed to keep up with them and, whenever it blew fresh, to pass them. By Lakes' standards she was not considered a good model, but it was admitted that she had 'a trig and neat appearance, not often found in vessels of her size,' and that she was 'by no means so tubby as the generality of English-built vessels.'

This engraving of the *Madeira Pet* appeared in the *Chicago Magazine* for August 1857. It was engraved from a photograph by the Chicago photographic artists Samuel D. Alschuler and Charles Florence. None of Alschuler's negatives are known to exist today.

Ships of Hastings

Hastings has been described as 'a port without any harbour to speak of'. Since its first recorded wooden pier was washed away in the reign of Elizabeth I, successive attempts to build a breakwater have fared badly against the rage of south-west gales. Hastings fishermen still beach their boats; almost to the end of the nineteenth century merchant vessels trading to Hastings did the same. The scene in this lithograph by John Thorpe was common enough in mid-century. A vessel loaded with coal has run up on the beach at high water springs; a gang of 'jumpers' are ready to whip out the cargo in baskets; the coal merchants' carts go to and fro' across the shingle; the horses wait as the carts are loaded. Off shore are smacks with chalk from the Holywell quarry at Eastbourne, bound for Rye. Holidaymakers watch the busy scene.

There were other animated sights on Hastings beach. In this aquatint by John Gendall shiprepairing and building go on under the Castle cliff in mid-century. The two vessels to the left with the characteristic lute sterns of the East Sussex beach boats are clearly fishermen. (Both of the principal Rye builders used this type of stern in a number of their schooners.) But the third vessel from the left appears to be a small merchant ship. Trading vessels were not only owned in Hastings, but they were built on and launched from this beach. For instance, the schooner *Wanderer*, 92 tons and 62ft long, was launched at Hastings in 1840 for a local owner.

One of these ships launched from Hastings beach was the schooner *Isabel*, 157 tons, shown here off Gibraltar going to windward in a stiff breeze. She was built at Hastings for J. & J. Adams of Pudding Lane, who were the largest importers of citrus fruits in the City of London. These fruit schooners were fast, weatherly craft designed to bring their perishable cargoes to market in the shortest possible time. To do this they were manned by small crews of daring seamen, who drove their little vessels to the limit. In the area covered by this book, fruiterers were built at Rye and by White at Cowes. In 1841 the *Isabel* was bringing oranges from the Azores to London; later that year when the orange season was over she went out from Liverpool to Newfoundland to load salt cod. In 1852 she was trading to Beirut.

A more humble type of Hastings trader was the *London* of Hastings. She was 92 tons, built at Chester in 1827, and was for many years in the Chester to London trade. By the 1860s she had been bought by Captain G. Robinson of St Leonards, where she occasionally brought coals from the North. As a youth Captain Robinson had been apprenticed to the master of the *London*, and he became her skipper at twenty-one.

Besides carrying coals from the North, the *London* carried china clay and grain and at times traded to Germany and the Low Countries. She was lost on the Yorkshire coast near Filey on 12 December 1883, bound from Hartlepool to Rye with coal.

The Brigs on the Beach

The shelving shingle beaches of south-east England are the homes of beach boats, hauled above high water mark by capstans. In the nineteenth century not only small fishing boats were beached. Merchantmen with cargoes came ashore at the top of spring tides, discharged their cargoes in one tide and were hauled off on the next. Rapidly growing holiday resorts had their coals brought from the North to be discharged on open beaches in this way but the list of a week's arrivals at Hastings in April 1850 shows that cargoes other than coal came by sea. The arrivals were—*Three Brothers*, from Portsmouth with potatoes; *William Pitt* from London with general cargo; *St Leonards* and *Milward* the same; *Jane* from London with deals; *Hope* from Goole with stone; *Maria* from Blyth with coals.

Some early examples of beaching come from Brighton. An engraving by George Cooke after H. Edridge shows a brig being unloaded on Brighton beach early in the nineteenth century. This little harbour was situated by the one-time Steyne opening, being protected to the westward by a natural shingle bank, which extended seawards for some 500 yards. The present Pool Valley depression is now the only evidence of this little haven. Coal was later beached between Ship Street and West Street, and it is said that some of the 'gaps' at Brighton perpetuate the tracks of the merchants' carts from the beach to their coal yards in the Kings Road.

The Cooke engraving shows very plainly how coal was discharged by 'jumping' or 'bell-roping'. A spar was rigged with a gin block; a wicker coal basket was bent to one end of a whip which ran through the gin and down to the deck where four ropes were attached; a stage with three or four steps was placed on deck by the hatch. This was the equipment.

Four men—the jumpers—each holding a rope, ran up the steps of the stage, pulling on the whip as they did so. This raised the filled basket some way from the bottom of the hold. Having reached the top of the stage, they paused an instant then jumped down on the deck together. The momentum of their combined weight jerked the full basket above the hatch coamings, where it was dexterously seized by the mate who ran with it to the side of the brig, quickly turned it over and tipped the contents down a shute over the vessel's side into a cart waiting below.

It was gruelling work for the jumpers, but it made for rapid discharge. With a good shovel gang in the hold the work went rapidly. It had to, for the vessel had to be unloaded and ballasted again with shingle in one tide. The danger points in the whole business were before the colliers came ashore and as they hauled off again. In either case an on-shore wind could mean disaster. This spirited sketch by John Constable captures the excitement of such a situation on Brighton beach. A squally wind blowing dead on shore, and three empty colliers rolling, pitching and falling aboard each other as their crews strain on the off warps to haul them clear of danger. It was just this sort of situation which ended beaching at Brighton. In October 1807 three coal brigs were wrecked on Brighton beach. After this a prohibitive insurance rate was imposed, and by 1830 the practice had ended.

33

Beaching continued at Hastings until 1879. Prominent among the Hastings collier brigs was the *Lamburn* launched on Hastings beach on 12 February 1833. This delightful picture of her discharging coal is full of detail. After carrying coal to Hastings for thirty-three years, the *Lamburn* was wrecked there on 18 November 1866—a short way from her building place.

Best remembered of the Hastings beach brigs was the *Pelican*. With her painted ports and pelican figurehead she was a distinctive sight. She too was built at Hastings in 1838. She was lost there in November 1879, after forty-one years of beach work. (They were long-lived those Hastings craft. One schooner, the *Bee*, built on the beach in 1828, was trading to the Azores forty years later.) This pencil sketch of the *Pelican* under sail shows what a picturesque little vessel she was after her conversion to a brig from her original schooner rig. The drawing was done for her owner Mr Ginner, a local coal merchant. What a grand picture it makes, the little brig bowling comfortably along before a fair wind. The wind is freshening and they are going to snug her down. The boy is going aloft to make fast the fore-topgallant; the Old Man is at the tiller and the cook is stoking up the galley fire to make tea.

Before it became compulsory for ships to display their names at bow and stern, a vessel's figurehead was sometimes the only clue to her identity. Once at Hartlepool, where the *Pelican* was waiting for coal, the foreman of the gang of trimmers came looking for her. He saw the figurehead and looked at it sadly puzzled. He scratched his head and turned to his mate.

'Is it a bird or ain't it a bird? Is it a bird or ain't it a bird? Is it—aye, it's a bird! Hey, *Pelican* ahoy!'

The *Pelican* was a favoured ship, accounted lucky and a legend in her own lifetime. Noted for her fast and regular passages under Captain James Dunk she is said to have once arrived at Hastings on four successive Saturdays with coals from Seaham—a truly remarkable achievement. So regular were her passages that in the latter part of her career, when sailing ships had to give way to steamers at the coal tips, the *Pelican* was always treated as a steamer and never had to wait her turn.

Any mid-Victorian view of Hastings is likely to show the *Pelican* moored off the Fishmarket, with an off-warp run off to a kedge, and discharging gear rigged. On the beach are some of the famous Hastings luggers, two-masted fully decked fishing boats. (As in the Deal luggers, p 17, the third mast was first unshipped and then finally dispensed with.)

Although the definition of the *Pelican* herself in this picture is poor, there is a great deal of fascinating detail in the rest of the photograph which must have been taken about 1870. This area is what an old guide book called 'this Ultima Thule of the unvisited end of the town'. Here in old Hastings was the quarter of the seafaring and the fishing community. The tarred fishermen's sheds, the luggers drawn up upon the shingle, the beach capstans and even the lines of washing all recall a long-vanished way of life. The little *Pelican*, moored a stone's throw from the water's edge provides a focus of interest. It is a point worth mentioning that some of the traders bringing cargoes to Hastings were so small that they, like the luggers, could be hauled up on the beach in an emergency.

This photograph of the *Pelican*, older but more sharply defined, shows details of the discharging gear. Not only is there a discharging gaff with a gin rigged on it, but from a spar between the masts a second gin is rigged. This would enable two baskets to be worked simultaneously, though obviously a second gang of men would have to be employed. It is just possible to distinguish the whip running through the second gin, terminating in the 'bellropes'.

After a quick passage from the North the *Pelican* would heave-to off Hastings and come ashore off the Fishmarket at high water. Her crew of four would have to work hard to get her moored, the sails stowed, the ship's boat off the hatch and in the water, hatches uncovered and discharging gear rigged. This is the state in which this picture shows her—ready for the merchant's carts to come alongside just as soon as the horses could get into the water. Even then the men's labours were not finished for they were expected to help work the cargo out. On one trip two teenage apprentices refused to work cargo, in an attempt to evade this irksome part of a coastwise sailor's job. A night in the police station was the result, and the next morning they were wielding their shovels in the hold.

In the mid-1870s the *Pelican's* rig was altered to a brigantine. The removal of the yards from the mainmast produced a rig less heavy on men and gear and hence more economical. This old engraving from the *Boy's Own Paper* shows the *Pelican* on the beach at the very end of her career. There is a stormy, threatening sky and the fishing luggers are coming in. This was what the crews of the beach brigs dreaded, an on-shore freshening wind when the time came to haul off.

One day in February 1850 the *Lamburn*, the *Queen* and the *Pelican* were all discharging coals on the beach. At low water it came on to blow hard from the SSW; before high water it was blowing a full gale. The *Lamburn* was hove off first on two hawsers, nearly made a wrong cast and all but went ashore again. The *Pelican* largest of the three, then hove off and while casting, carried away her jibboom against the *Queen's* stern. The *Queen* was a small vessel, so small that it was possible to haul her up on the beach.

Equally frustrating was an on-shore wind when a collier arrived. In January 1850 ten sail of Hastings colliers arrived together from the North. Scarcely had they anchored than the wind shifted. All ten had to heave up and run back to the Downs for shelter.

On 11 November 1879 the *Pelican* came ashore on the morning tide and discharged her coal as usual. She was being hauled off in the darkness of a November evening when the off warp upon which the crew were heaving, suddenly parted. A stiff on-shore breeze was blowing, and the *Pelican* was quickly thrown broadside on the beach where she remained all night with the seas breaking over her.

This photograph shows her situation the next morning, and pretty unpleasant it looks! Her port bulwarks had been torn away by the seas and her whole hull was badly strained. The hawser which had parted, appeared, on examination, to have been partially cut through by some malicious person, (a disgruntled member of the crew?). Although a £10 reward was offered by the police for information, none was forthcoming.

The following weekend the ballast was taken out of the *Pelican*; on the next spring tide she was refloated and towed round to Rye. Examination proved her too badly damaged for repair. She was later broken up, and since then there have been no colliers on Hastings beach.

At Eastbourne too, colliers came ashore on the beach. One was the *Bee* of Hull, under the command of Captain Parker. In the early 1930s when I was collecting information about her, there were still old fishermen who could recall her. Even in 1971 her anchor, upon which she hauled off, was still in position, though covered by sand. The *Bee* was tiny, 58 tons, and built at Hull in 1837. In this very old photograph she appears to have been a typical East coast collier, very bluff in the bows, a straight stem with no fancywork in the shape of a figurehead and with a generally old-fashioned air about her. She brought coal for a Mr Vine whose yard was in Seaside. She used to come ashore at a point opposite St Aubyn's Road, and directly the water was low enough, work would begin.

This ancient photograph gives yet another variation of discharging arrangements. The small boat is hoisted up on end to the foremast to get it clear of the hatch; a shute is rigged over the side; and the discharging gaff is rigged with a spar to support it.

This practice of unloading cargoes on open beaches is an extremely ancient one; it is mentioned in the Icelandic sagas. Nowhere was it carried out in more spectacular fashion than on the beaches of nineteenth-century Sussex.

Ships of a Sussex River

The Sussex Ouse winds sluggishly along its muddy bed on its course to the sea. From Lewes to the coast it was navigable not only by barges of a primitive rig which sailed, were poled or merely drifted along, but also by small sea-going ships. This early nineteenth-century picture gives the 'feel' of river activity at Lewes, with barges and the timber yard where small ships were built. The barge in the foreground has been credited by the artist with a totally superfluous gaff. It was really a spritsail barge, something like the Arun barge on page 86. In medieval times the Ouse had entered the sea at Seaford, but the ancient village of Meeching became the New Haven when the river altered its course overnight; so that Newhaven grew up at the Ouse's new and more westerly mouth. Shipbuilding was carried on there from the seventeenth century. After 1731 when the pier protecting the mouth of the Ouse was repaired, Newhaven's fortunes prospered. As early as 1753 a ship, the *Lewes*, was built at Lewes for the Barbados sugar trade, in 1784 the ship *Jamaica Planter*, 400 tons, was launched at Newhaven for the West Indies trade.

The river's great years of maritime activity were in the nineteenth century. In 1865 eighteen sailing ships were owned in the port of Newhaven, fourteen in the town itself, three in Lewes and one in East Grinstead. At Lewes was Rickman & Godlee's yard, later Chatfield's (top opposite). The first sea-going ship to be launched at Lewes in the nineteenth century was the *Lewes Castle* in 1839; (bottom opposite); the last was the *Wallands* of 1866, (page 44). At Newhaven John Gray began building ships about 1840, and the last ship built at Newhaven, the *Blonde*, was launched by Tolman in 1874. Here is a delightful example of a Lewes ship in a little dock beside two flint-built cottages at Lewes. On the evidence of her figurehead she is probably the brig *Eagle*, 142 tons built by Chatfield in 1863. Whatever her name, she is very much the old-timer; the whisker boom, the single topsails clewed up to the quarters of the yards; the 'pig's ears' hanging on each side of the bunt would soon be old-fashioned even in 1863.

42

Chatfield's timber yard beside the railway at Lewes in the 1860s. Amid the profusion of detail—tree trunks, timber carriages, and sheer-legs—there is a vessel in frame (left). She could be the *Richard and Emily* (1862), the *Eagle* (1863) or the *Wallands* (1866).

This lithograph shows the launching of the tiny brig *Lewes Castle*, 61 tons, in March 1839, from the yards of Rickman & Godlee. A the usual post-launch party held at the Star Inn, the toast was drunk to, 'The *Lewes Castle*', may she make prosperous voyages and profitable freights!'

Another Lewes-built ship was the brigantine *Harriett*, 182 tons, of 1848. Launched above the bridge without topsides she was towed downstream for completion. In 1861 she was sliced in half horizontally and given a deeper draught. For over forty years she brought coal to Newhaven for Lewes merchants until she went ashore on the Yorkshire coast on 18 November 1893.

The *Wallands*, a topsail schooner, was launched by Chatfield in 1866, the last ship built at Lewes, for Goldfinch of Faversham. She is reputed to have carried the last cargo of oak treenails, used for fastening wooden ships, from Lewes to the Baltic.

In the 1860s the quays of Newhaven were thronged with colliers bringing coal for the cross-Channel packets and gas and house-coal for nearby towns. But other steamers whose livelihood depended on sailing ships frequented the port. These were tugboats from the London River, in particular Watkins' tugs from Gravesend, which ventured this far down Channel in search of homeward-bound sailing ships. Watkins' tugs found Newhaven a convenient base, and put in for coal and provisions. Watkins even had a barque the *Watkins*, 288 tons, built by Gray the Newhaven shipbuilder. She was one of the great fleet of Forty-niners at San Francisco at the time of the gold rush.

The tug in the left-centre is almost certainly Watkins' famous *Uncle Sam*. Her twin funnels, side by side, are an easily recognisable feature. Built by R. & H. Green of Blackwall, builders of the famed Blackwall frigates, the *Uncle Sam* was launched in 1848. This tug which towed so many crack clipper ships in and out of the London River, was one of the most widely known ships of the nineteenth century. Relegated to river work in her old age, she was a favoured tug for berthing the P & O liners. She is said to have been the first merchant ship to have passed under Tower Bridge when it was opened in 1894. She was broken up in 1900.

At Cheddleton Flint Mill near Stoke-on-Trent, a preservation trust has rescued and re-stored the last surviving flint-crushing mill. In the mid-eighteenth century English potters began to add flint to their earthenware composition to improve its whiteness. To make it easy to crush it was burnt in special kilns, and then ground with water in a pan mill, where large stones powered by water wheels were driven round over a pavement of smaller stones.

Here is the raw material of the process. Beach boats like the *Albertine* in the foreground were run on to the Sussex beaches to collect rounded flint pebbles locally known as 'bould-ers'. The open yawl-rigged boats which did this work were known as 'boulder boats'. They brought their cargoes into Newhaven, where the stones were landed until a sufficient quan-tity had been accumulated to load a coaster like the *Sussex Maid* or the brig *Aldersons* (built at Sunderland in 1865 and owned in Southampton). Ships like these would take the stones to Runcorn where they would be offloaded again into narrow boats which took them to the Pot-teries. This picture taken in the 1870s illustrates a piece of vanished industrial history.

Originally a brig, the *Sussex Maid* was launched by Gray in 1856 for Chatfield of Lewes. In 1862 she was trading to the Mediterranean; in 1870 to the West Indies. George Robinson, a Newhaven shipchandler, bought her in the early seventies and rerigged her as a brigantine. He ran her in the coal trade until his death in 1903. Here she is at Newhaven ready to discharge.

About 1840 a young shipbuilder, John Gray, acquired the small shipyard at Newhaven. He had served his apprenticeship in a Yarmouth yard and was familiar with the latest design and construction techniques. Gray expanded the yard, which had hitherto dealt mainly with repair work. Supplies of Sussex oak could be brought by barge down the Ouse, which also connected him with the iron foundry at Lewes. He began by building small, fast vessels for the Madeira trade and by the end of the decade his reputation was established. In December 1848 when he launched the barque *Alice Maud*, 250 tons, he had no less than five vessels building or fitting out, with an aggregate tonnage of 1,000 tons.

Gray was a sophisticated builder who worked from properly drawn plans—his draught for the *Watkins* is among the plans in the National Maritime Museum—and he specialised in small wooden brigs and barques of under 500 tons. In January 1850 he launched the barque *Corsair's Bride* for Jonathan Clark of London, the owner of the *Alice Maud*. Both these vessels were for the Algoa Bay trade. She was followed by the *John Gray*, which he himself used for the Mediterranean trade. In 1851 he built the barque *Don Ricardo* for Liverpool owners for the South American trade. Later that year came the steamer *Paoun Shun* for Dent & Co, of Canton, the well-known China merchants. She was the first steamer built in Sussex and at the time the largest schooner-rigged vessel in the world.

Typical of the small square-riggers which Gray turned out was the barque *Lewes*, 248 tons, which he launched in 1855 for Messrs Chatfield & Sampson of Newhaven. She was built for the Mediterranean trade and in the painting below she is seen entering the port of Smyrna. With her Red Ensign, signal flags, name pennant and Masonic flag, this is a colourful example of the type of ship portraits done in Mediterranean ports at this period.

The story behind this pair of ship portraits is unusual. The *Lewes* was anchored in the roads off Beirut in the great gale of January 1859 when seventeen ships were driven ashore after their cables parted. When the gale began, Captain W. Bennett of the *Lewes* had already prudently sent down topgallant and royal yards and determined to ride out the storm with both anchors down. In the heavy rolling sea the port chain parted at 90 fathoms. Fearing that the other cable would not hold, Captain Bennett made preparations to slip and to attempt to force his way offshore against the gale. He slipped the starboard chain at 60 fathoms and under a jib, two spencers and a close-reefed maintopsail he worked the *Lewes* out of danger. The fore topsail and the mainsail blew away, leaving a few shreds of canvas streaming from the yards. For his great exertions in saving the *Lewes*, Captain Bennett was awarded £20 by the underwriters; with some of this money he had these two pictures painted by Raffaele Corsini of Smyrna to record his little ship in her glory and her adversity.

Soon after this the *Lewes* was converted to a brig. She was wrecked in 1866.

A typical Mediterranean trader was the brig *John Hillman*, 237 tons, built by Gray in 1852 and named after her owner. Ships of this size and rig comprised a high proportion of the British merchant fleet at this period. The *John Hillman* sailed in the South American and Mediterranean trades. The legend beneath this painting states that she was entering the port of Palermo under Captain G. T. Williams in February 1856. Marine artists of varying degrees of ability practised in many Mediterranean ports at this time, producing hundreds of colourful and technically accurate ship-portraits for ship-proud masters and owners. The *John Hillman* was out of Lloyd's Register in 1869.

The *Amanda* (opposite) comes towards the end of Newhaven's sailing ship years. She was a collier owned by G. Robinson, and his son Captain J. R. Robinson became master of her in the 1890s at the age of twenty-two. The *Amanda* was launched at Portmadoc in 1864. At the ceremony, the cradle collapsed when she was halfway down the slipway so that she was launched on to dry land! Eventually she was floated off and sailed for many years in the slate trade out of Portmadoc. Here she is entering Lowestoft under tow. Captain Robinson sold her in 1903 and she was lost on the Crossand near Yarmouth in 1905.

The Bull Line of Newhaven

In the early 1880s John Bull of Newhaven and his cousin N. C. Bull set up at 25 South Road as shipbrokers and shipowners. The first ships of the Bull Line to fly the house flag of the bull's head, were four second-hand vessels; the brig *Carbonaria*, the snow *Commerce*, the barquentine *Emily Smeed* and the brigantine *Fannie C*. On the death of N. C. Bull the business became known as J. H. Bull & Co. John Bull held the Eastbourne Gas Co's contract for bringing gas coal from the north to Newhaven. At various times the Bull Line owned eighteen ships. Although they visited other parts of the coast and occasionally went to the Baltic, they were best known in the coal trade. By the end of the 1890s sailing colliers were being driven out by steamers to which they had to give way at the coal tips. John Bull continued in business partly through sentiment for he was a real lover of sail, even though ships such as his were becoming old and uneconomic to manage. After his death in about 1907 the five remaining ships of his fleet were sold. The firm is still in business though not as shipowners.

The *Carbonaria*, 301 tons, was built by May at Shoreham in 1867. John Bull sold her to become a barge, (top opposite).

The *Commerce*, 260 tons, was launched by Balley at Shoreham in 1862. In this painting she is passing the *Carbonaria*. At first glance both vessels are apparently brigs but the *Commerce* has a small trysail mast just aft of the mainmast, which makes her strictly speaking a snow.

(Below) John Bull with some of his captains and office staff.

The *Emily Smeed* (top opposite) and the *Fannie C* completed John Bull's original quartet. The barquentine *Emily Smeed*, 299 tons, built by Smeed at Sittingbourne in 1872, was an attempt to develop the barge hull in larger craft. The big Smeed barges—there were two barquentines, a brigantine and a barque—carried 5-600 tons of coal, could come out over the bars of the coal ports at neap tides, and would make their light passages with little or no ballast. Lord Runciman wrote in his *Collier Brigs* that they 'would show the notorious coasters the road with the wind between the masts, on the quarter or right aft; but beating to windward with a jumpy sea, they sagged badly to leeward, notwithstanding the help of their ponderous leeboards.' Judging by this painting made after she became a unit of the Bull Line, the *Emily Smeed* had by then dispensed with her leeboards. John Bull sold her to Aberdeen in 1903.

The *Fannie C*, 316 tons, was a brigantine built in New Brunswick in 1880. John Bull sold her to the Italians in 1887. Notice the ponderous wooden stock of the anchor on the rail and the interesting sprit-rigged vessel the other side of the foremast. Unlike most of the English-built brigs and brigantines, the *Fannie C* does not have a Bentinck boom below the foreyard.

The *John Bull* bought in the 1890s was a small topsail schooner originally the *Hugh Barclay*, built by Barclay of Ardrossan in 1870. She remained in the Bull Line until its dispersal (above).

55

The *Merchant*, 282 tons, and the *Pennine*, 296 tons (above), joined the Bull Line in the late 1880s. The *Merchant* built by May at Shoreham in 1869 was a brig with a striking full length male figurehead. She was the only English ship in Constanza when the Russians entered that port in 1877 in the Russo-Turkish War; a time when Anglo-Russian relations were at a low ebb. 'With all those murderous looking Russians around we never knew what would happen next. The soldiers used to swarm all over the ship and rigging,' an old sailor who was aboard at the time, once told me. The *Pennine* in the centre of the picture, was a snow built at Sunderland in 1867. She was lost in Yarmouth Roads in 1897 with only one survivor.

First ship to join the Bull Line and the last to go was the old *Commerce* (opposite). John Bull's executors sold her in 1906. She was the last sailing ship on the coast with the old-fashioned deep single topsails. Here she is towing in between the piers at Newhaven at the turn of the century. After she was sold she became a barge at Yarmouth and Milford Haven, and finally an undecked lighter at Birkenhead. Stripped of all her fittings she was a familiar sight in the West Float; her massive construction was still evident, so were the traces of some incised lines of scrollwork round her bows. The *Commerce* was broken up in 1946—the last of the wooden Sussex square-riggers.

Shoreham Square-riggers

In 1874, there were 161 sailing ships, mostly barques and brigs, owned in the port of Shoreham. Of these eighty-eight had been built there. By 1909 not one Shoreham-built sailing ship was still trading. In their noontide the Shoreham barques and brigs were to be found all over the globe. There were many small shipowners owning one or two vessels and these accounted for most of the 119 sailing ships owned in Shoreham in 1865. The principal owners were R. H. Penney 10 ships, T. E. Gates 25, H. Adams 3, and W. Banfield 3. The Shoreham shipbuilders were James Britton Balley at the Old Shipyard (1838 to 1863); John May and T. Thwaites at Kingston (1838 to 1871); William May at the Old Shipyard (1865 to 1874); John Shuttleworth at the Canal Shipyard (1862 to 1874); and Dyer & Son at the Old yard (1875 to 1878). Between them they must have built several hundred ships.

Much of Shoreham's nineteenth-century maritime prosperity resulted from its proximity to the growing resort of Brighton, and to the construction of the dock or canal from Southwick to Aldrington Basin. This was opened on the 20 February 1855 when the brig *George*, 158 tons was the first ship to enter the lock gates. This ancient photograph dates from then. She is an old-timer, bluff and beamy, with deep single topsails and great wooden stocked anchors. May & Thwaites launched her at Kingston in 1839. After a long and grimy career as a collier, she was sold to Whitby owners in 1861 and wrecked near Hornsea in 1882.

The mid-century 'new look' in wooden shipbuilding is noticeable in the snow *Agricola*, one of four almost standard vessels launched by Balley in 1862. The others were the *Commerce*, *Shamrock* and *Cambria*. The *Agricola* was built for the carriage of grain from the Mediterranean, the Black Sea and the River Plate. She registered 278 tons and carried 600 tons. Her owner Henry Adams was a miller. She was a typical ocean tramp of the 1860s. Twenty years later she was becoming too small for deep-water work, and John Bull of Newhaven bought her in 1887 for the coal trade. She dropped out of the Register about 1904, Here she is at the turn of the century on the patent slip at Newhaven, a photograph which shows very well the complicated cat's cradle that was the running rigging of a brig or snow.

A smaller vessel of the same rig was the *Sarah*, 185 tons, built by May & Thwaites in 1862 for W. Banfield, the Brighton coal merchant. Named for and launched by his daughter, he owned the *Sarah* for over thirty years. This little brig, with two royals and topmast and lower studdingsails, was tiller steered. Her master all this time was Captain W. Baker who came out of the Hastings beach collier *Midge* to take command of Banfield's brig *Ebenezer* when that ship was launched in 1860. He took over the *Sarah* when she was new. He was a skilful coasting seaman and a hard driver who nevertheless kept his crew year after year. With his top hat, his green velveteen waistcoat and his churchwarden pipe, Billy Baker was a character—and he knew it!

John McCoy remembered sighting the *Sarah* in the 1870s. 'It was a good passage from the Baltic across the North Sea. At the Kentish Knock we spoke a northern-bound brig the *Sarah* of Shoreham, stunsails set. We had a head wind and she a fair one, and I remember one of the men saying that we should not get a fair wind until the *Sarah* arrived in the North, as her master, Captain Baker, always carried the wind with him.' The *Sarah* was sold to Littlehampton in 1895 and was hulked in 1910.

60

One of the ocean-wandering barques from Shoreham was the *Eurus*, 327 tons, built by John Shuttleworth in 1870 for Henry Adams. John McCoy recalled a three year voyage beginning in 1882. 'Out of a ship and walking round the London Dock, I saw a smart little barque with painted ports. I went and looked under her stern and saw she was a Sussex vessel —the *Eurus* of Shoreham. I went on board to speak to the captain and asked him if he wanted any hands. He looked at me and turning his hands over, he said with a laugh, "I've got two good ones here which are all I require". I asked him if he wanted any ABs, and he said, "Well, we won't be ready for a week". I said I could wait that long. He said I would have to sign on for three years to which I agreed. We went out in the autumn of 1882 and made a quick passage of 46 days to Algoa Bay. The *Eurus* was the best ship I had been in so far. We were a crew of twelve. She was kept like a yacht and Captain Haynes was a good master. We left Algoa Bay for the Mauritius where we loaded sugar for Adelaide.' In the next three years this small ship visited Adelaide, Durban, Calcutta, Mauritius, Adelaide, Newcastle NSW, and New Zealand. Adams sold the *Eurus* to John Bull in 1887.

R. Dyer built the barque *Britannia*, 464 tons, at the Old Shipyard for Cheeseman Bros in 1877. Launched with her masts standing, she was completed alongside the yard. Under Captain Alfred Gasston with his wife and two children and a crew of fifteen, she ranged the oceans for only six years. She was lost on Sable Island in September 1883. Thirteen lives were lost including those of Mrs Gasston and her children—an all too common nineteenth-century sea tragedy.

When Dyer launched the *Osman Pacha* in 1878, she was to be the last square-rigger built in Shoreham. Named for the Turkish victor of the battles of Plevna in 1877, her figurehead was 'an Arab with a turban on the head dress, and a sash with a dagger on the body'. Never owned in Shoreham, she sailed out of London, Liverpool and Glasgow in the Mauritius trade. In 1890 a typical voyage was London, New York, Algoa Bay, Mauritius, Melbourne. One who sailed in her then wrote to me in 1935, 'We only manned her pumps every twenty-four hours and then she would suck after fifteen to twenty minutes. Those who built her had something to be proud of. Ten to twelve knots were common for the Old Girl, but on one occasion while running our easting down from the Mauritius the Old Man knocked fourteen knots out of her, and damned near made a mess of her and the whole crew.'

The *Osman Pacha* went missing in the Indian Ocean in 1892, still commanded by the same sail-carrying captain.

Penney's 'Stars'

The firm of R. H. Penney & Sons is an example of a shipowner with small local beginnings increasing the scope of his business until his Shoreham-registered ships were known in the most distant ports of the world.

In 1822 Edward Lucas of Southwick, a shipowner in a small way, took over the business of a corn and coal merchant. In connection with this business he owned and operated six small ships. One of these was the schooner *Kingston*, 105 tons, the first of May & Thwaites' ships to be launched from their Kingston yard in 1838. A pair of delightful watercolours of her entering and leaving Valetta, by the Maltese marine artist Nicholas S. Cammillieri, is still in the possession of a descendant of Edward Lucas (opposite). Another of the original six was the snow *Jessamine*, 196 tons, built at Sunderland in 1840 (centre vessel below).

In 1852 Lucas handed over his business to his son-in-law Robert Horne Penney, whose family came from Poole. Penney steadily increased his fleet. Six wooden barques which he ordered from local shipyards in 1863-5 began the series of astronomical names, most of them beginning with the letter A, which became such a feature of the Penney fleet. By the end of the 1860s he was ordering his first iron ships from the north of England. In the 1870s he bought his first steamers. By 1895 he had very sensibly sold all his sailing ships. The firm continued to own steamers up to World War II and are still in business where they began, at Southwick, as shipbrokers and wharfingers.

The first ship Robert Penney had specially built for himself (as opposed to buying second-hand tonnage) was the wooden brig *Blue Bell*, 198 tons, which J. B. Balley launched for him in 1854 at a cost of £2,558 (below). In the photograph on the previous page the *Blue Bell* is the vessel on the right. The contrast between her and the tubby old *Jessamine* emphasises the changes that had taken place in shipbuilding fashions in sixteen years. This picture was taken inside the lock gates at Southwick and it is probable that the two brigs in the background are units of the Penney fleet.

Balley launched two three-masted schooners in 1856, the *Wild Dayrell* (named after the 1855 Derby winner) for local owners and the *Osprey*, 220 tons, for Robert Penney. These are early examples of the three-masted schooner rig in southern England, though another, the *Lamplighter*, had been launched at Rye the year before. The *Wild Dayrell* was described as 'of Yankee three-mast schooner rig', ie a fore-and-aft schooner rig without square topsails. She was not an immediate success and on her maiden voyage carried away all her gaffs and booms. The *Osprey* (above) cost Penney £3,164. She was heavily rigged with lofty topmasts and her owner always spoke of her as a fast sailer. She carried not only a fore royal—exceptional for a topsail schooner—but she even set royal studdingsails. Her master, Captain Poole, came to her out of the old *Jessamine* and after remaining in the *Blue Bell* for some years came ashore to become marine superintendent of the greatly expanded Penney fleet. The firm always had an extremely good name as an employer. Men signed on aboard their ships for voyage after voyage, while masters often remained in the same ship for a decade and sometimes for two. The *Osprey* was lost on the Scottish coast in 1868.

In 1863-8, Robert Penney had nine new barques built, two by May & Thwaites, four by John Shuttleworth, and one each in Cardiff, Portsmouth and Sunderland. This was the scene in Shuttleworth's yard at Southwick in 1864. The *Capella*, 246 tons, is fitting out and appears almost ready for sea. The *Arcturus*, 279 tons, is nearly ready for launching; and, just visible on the extreme right, the *Astrea* is in frame; three ocean tramps of the sixties. John Shuttleworth was in his late twenties when he began shipbuilding. His efforts to compete with iron shipbuilding in the North were dogged by ill-health and he was dead at forty-three.

Penney's first iron ship was the barque *Cora Linn*, 468 tons, which he bought in 1867. She had been built by Pearse at Stockton in 1866 and had already made a voyage to Hong Kong when Penney bought her for £8,886. Under Captain T. Glazebrook she continued to trade to the East Indies. Here photographed in about 1870 in the Sarawak River, the *Cora Linn* appears in the setting of a Conrad novel. The awnings stretched over the decks and the utterly still water suggest humid, oppressive heat, without a breath of air. The lonely wharf, the muddy foreshore, the native schooner alongside the *Cora Linn*, the decaying thatched go-downs and the omnipresent jungle suggest Conrad so strongly, that one looks for Almayer or for Tom Lingard's brig. In 1876 the *Cora Linn* grounded and capsized on the Old Warp Sand in the Humber while being towed up to Goole, and the master's wife, her two children and an apprentice were all drowned.

The *Altair*, 397 tons, and the *Lyra*, 388 tons, were the first iron ships specially built for Robert Penney. They were launched at Sunderland by Iliff, Mounsey & Co in 1867. The *Altair* was sold in 1879; the *Lyra* in 1893. The *Lyra* was once brought home around the Horn under jury rig after being dismasted in the South Pacific.

The *Alcestis*, 1868 (398 tons), *Asterion*, 1869 (508 tons), and *Auriga*, 1869 (578 tons) were the next three iron barques which Iliff, Mounsey & Co built for Robert Penney. The *Auriga* (above) traded to New Zealand for many years. She was later owned there and was employed in the Mauritius and inter-colonial trade. She became a hulk at Melbourne in 1912 and was broken up in 1930.

The two pictures of the *Asterion* (next page) could have been taken any time between 1887 and 1899 when she made ten voyages to Nelson out of a total of fifteen New Zealand voyages. Like her sisters and like the Penney barques which followed them in the seventies, the *Asterion* was under charter for many years to the Shaw, Savill Co. Most of them had their 'tween decks pierced for ports so that they could carry emigrants. These two pictures are splendid period pieces. Towed into port by a vintage tug with a steadying sail, this little Sussex barque has sailed half way round the world to be greeted by a man with a buggy, and by a straw-hatted boy with a dog. The *Asterion* was sold to Shaw, Savill & Co in the eighties and to the Swedes at the end of the century.

The three Penney barques of 1875 were the *Alastor,* 823 tons, the *Alpheta,* 817 tons, and the *Antares,* 820 tons. This picture of the *Antares* taken at Lyttleton in 1878 has all the appeal of Longfellow's 'A boy's will is the wind's will, and the thoughts of youth are long, long thoughts'; and of the same poet's word picture of 'sailors with bearded lips, and the beauty and mystery of the ships'. The *Antares,* 196ft long, is small enough by modern standards. The figures on the fo'c'slehead give the scale. This evocative photograph recalls all the atmosphere of the small deep-waterman before ships became monsters out of scale with the men aboard them. The iron hull, only a generation away from wooden ships, the graceful spars, the well-kept rigging, the barbed dolphin striker, the finely carved figurehead, the elaborate trail-boards and the lion-faced cathead all contribute something to the enjoyable atmosphere of this picture.

Under Captain A. Lewis she made nine voyages to New Zealand with emigrants. She had a reputation for speed. On one occasion she is said to have logged 17 knots. Her best passage out to New Zealand was 91 days and she once came home in 74 days. Sold to the Norwegians in 1894, she was lost in 1910.

The 'Alastor' New Zealand Emigrant Ship

An ancient faded photograph, but she sets a main skysail yard! The *Alastor* launched by Mounsey & Foster (successors to Iliff, Mounsey & Co) at Sunderland in 1875, was Robert Penney's last and largest sailing ship. She was ordered and built during that short period in the early seventies when sailing ships were competing successfully against steamers. The year 1875 was a peak for sailing ship launchings and the crest of a minor boom for sail. These were large new iron sailing vessels, not so heavily rigged in proportion to size as some of the earlier wooden ships of the sixties, but with much greater carrying capacity. The *Alastor* was a barque of that tough puddled iron which frequently outlasted steel. She was the only Shoreham vessel ever to carry a skysail. Her first suit of sails, made at Penney's sail loft in Southwick, were the largest ever made there.

The construction of the three ships at Sunderland was supervised for the owner by the senior master of the Penney fleet, Captain Thomas Glazebrook, who was to command the *Alastor* for twenty years. With her 'tween decks pierced for portholes she was intended for the New Zealand emigrant business; usually under charter to Shaw, Savill & Co, whose houseflag she flies in the photograph opposite.

Between 1877 and 1890 she made ten New Zealand voyages, sometimes returning to the UK with wheat from San Francisco or antimony ore from Borneo. It was often said that Captain Glazebrook and the *Alastor* were as well known in New Zealand ports as they were in Shoreham. In November 1880 she left London for Wellington with a general cargo and twenty-nine passengers—small farmers, labourers and their families. While she was running down her easting her wheel was smashed by a following sea which swept her poop. An improvised wheel was contrived but the *Alastor* had to be shortened down to lower topsails. She arrived at Wellington 125 days out from London.

This contemporary painting shows the *Alastor* outward-bound off the South Foreland. Consider her scale as compared to that of the *Antares* (p 73), and one realises what an extremely attractive little vessel she was. Here she flies Penney's red star houseflag with a blue border. Her pronounced sheer forward is very noticeable; so is the big deckhouse and the monkey-poop aft.

Captain Glazebrook is said to have sailed round the world fifteen times in the *Alastor* and in other ships he commanded. Early in 1888 the *Alastor* loaded antimony ore in Borneo for the UK. On 28 February in the Indian Ocean her cargo shifted in a typhoon and she was almost completely dismasted. Captain Glazebrook and his crew got to work, righted the cargo, improvised a jury rig and brought her into Port Louis, Mauritius, where this photograph was taken. At that time Port Louis was well equipped for dealing with disabled sailing ships. New spars were sent out from England and the *Alastor* was re-rigged. In 1891, when she was at Santos in Brazil, Captain Glazebrook and all his crew went down with yellow fever from which six men died. In 1894 she suffered weather damage outward bound round the Horn. She put into Valpariso for repairs. Here Captain Glazebrook contracted typhoid, and the mate took the ship home. By this time only the *Alastor* remained of the Penney sailing fleet. In 1895 R. H. Penney & Sons sold her to a Norwegian owner.

Her Norwegian owner, M. F. Stray, kept the *Alastor* in general trade and made a great deal of money out of her in World War I. On one occasion the Royal Navy brought her into Lerwick with a contraband cargo on board. In the early twenties she was in the logwood trade from the West Indies to France. From 1925 to 1928 under another Norwegian owner the old ship came down to the 'firewood' trade from the Gulf of Bothnia to the UK, carrying short lengths of timber—the offcuts of the sawmills—used in cheap furniture and packing cases. In these years the *Alastor* lost her figurehead as well as her skysail and royals.

In 1928 she was sold to a Finnish owner Consul Karl Schröder of Hango. She usually made from two to five trips to London or a South Coast port every season, though in the slump year of 1931 she made only one. In 1934 she made her last trip too late in the season to get back to Finland before the ice closed, and her master Captain Julius Erikson laid her up at Tollesbury in Essex for the winter. This photograph shows her appearance at this period.

Both of these deck views were taken aboard the *Alastor* during her visits to England in the thirties. The picture opposite is taken from the mainmast looking aft to the poop. At the entrance to the accommodation was the builder's brass plate—'Mounsey & Foster-No 76. 1875. Iron Ship Builders—South Dock, Sunderland'. Aft of the mainmast is visible the main fife rail and the flywheel of the pumps. Behind the fife rail a deck capstan is just visible. The capstan bars are in a stand beneath the lifeboat.

The picture on this page is taken from the fo'c'slehead. The deckhouse aft of the foremast would contain the crew's quarters and the galley. Notice how in these pictures the ratlines of the rigging have been replaced by wooden battens.

As the storm clouds gathered over Europe in the late thirties the *Alastor* continued to sail —still classed 100A1 at Lloyd's.

In 1937 and 1938 the *Alastor* visited Portsmouth and Plymouth. In December 1938 she was in serious trouble off Aberdeen and had to be towed to safety by a harbour tug. At the outbreak of war in 1939 she was in England. She was laid up never to sail again. In 1941 when Finland entered the war on the German side, she was seized by the authorities. For the rest of the war she was used by the Royal Navy as an accommodation ship, lying off Burnham-on-Crouch. Adrian Small photographed her here in 1946, with topgallant masts and yards sent down (opposite).

Later in 1946 the *Alastor* was towed to Ramsgate to become a floating restaurant. Tarted up with painted ports she became *The Bounty* aboard which the holidaymaker could buy snacks and play the pintables and slot machines. In March 1951 she left this degrading set-up to be towed up the Thames. She spent some time at Rotherhithe being fitted up to be an attraction in the Festival of Britain. The promoters' plans went wrong, and early in 1952 she was broken up at Grays.

Writing with hindsight is seems incredible that this delightful little barque was ever allowed to disappear.

Littlehampton and Arundel

In 1865 thirty-five sailing vessels were registered in the port of Arundel, which then included Littlehampton. Eight were schooners, the rest were brigs or barques. T. Isemonger was the principal shipowner and in the early nineteenth century a shipbuilder too. On 15 May 1866 Henry Harvey launched the brig *Emma* from his Clymping yard for Brighton owners for the River Plate trade. She was 291 tons, and launched fully rigged, sails bent and ready for sea. The vessel ahead of her with yards cockbilled is the brig *Mitchell Grove*, built at Arundel in 1815. She was the vessel which rescued the sole survivor of the *Dalhousie* (page 102). She was still afloat in 1873 officially described as 'a chronically diseased old tub not fit to go to sea'.

Littlehampton became a port of registry in 1869. Henry Harvey began building ships at the Clymping yard in 1848 and his sons were launching wooden deep-watermen until 1880 —the last being the barque *Goodwood*, 535 tons. She would have been similar to the *Gratitude*, 544 tons, of 1876, (top opposite) here seen in her later rig of a barquentine.

In the eighties and nineties several ketch barges with leeboards were launched. This series of barges continued into the twentieth century, the last appearing in 1919. One was the *Clymping* (below), 121 tons, built in 1909. She was 93ft long with a 23ft beam and only 8.3ft depth of hold. Here she is alongside Harvey's yard with a big Baltic schooner on one of the four slips. In 1930 the *Clymping*, with another Harvey ketch barge, the *Leading Light* (1906), and the Faversham *Goldfinch* (page 10), crossed the Atlantic in thirty-eight days for work on the Berbice River in British Guiana.

This was the *Ebenezer*, Littlehampton's last sailing ship, owned by the Robinson family and commanded by Captain Louis Robinson for thirteen years. Built as a brig by May at Shoreham in 1860, she was one of four colliers owned by Banfield & Co, the Brighton coal merchants (page 60 and 107). In the great easterly gale of 12-13 November 1901, while commanding the brigantine *Constance Ellen* Captain Robinson failed to get between the piers at South Shields. Because of the ebb tide and the fact that the ship had carried away some of her sails, he had very little control of her. He put her helm hard up and ran her ashore at the back of South Shields pier where she became a total loss, though Captain Robinson and his crew were rescued by the rocket apparatus of the local Volunteer Life Brigade.

Captain Robinson next went master of the *Ebenezer*, converted by then to a brigantine (above), until she was sold in 1915. He once left Grimsby in her at 9.30 am and arrived at Littlehampton at 9.30 pm the next day. Once he sailed the *Ebenezer* home from Hartlepool five times within one month.

After Captain Robinson sold the *Ebenezer* she was sunk by a German submarine in 1917. The story was that as the U-boat began firing, the *Ebenezer's* Irish skipper ran up on deck in his stockinged feet shouting loudly, 'Stop firing, we're neutral!'

Captain Louis Robinson died in 1962, aged eighty-six. In his will he left £3,500 in four per cent Consols to the South Shields Volunteer Life Brigade, without whose services sixty-one years before 'I would not have been here to accumulate what I have now decided to try to dispose of.'

The railway bridge over the Arun at Ford was permanently closed in 1937. But sea-going vessels were still arriving at Arundel at the beginning of the present century. Here the Littlehampton paddle-tug *Jumna* (built 1884) is towing a big loaded ketch to a berth almost below the aristocratic walls of the castle.

QUEENHITHE *Wharf,*
UPPER THAMES STREET.

SEWARD & Co.'s
Canal Barges
LOAD EVERY
Wednesday and Saturday,
FOR

ARUNDEL,
CHICHESTER, WORTHING,

Amberley	Billingshurst	Emsworth	Little Hampton	Petworth	Steyning
Angmering	Bognor	Havant	Midhurst	Pulbro'	Yapton

and all adjacent and intermediate Places.
ALSO **REGULAR BARGES** TO

Henley, Marlow, Newbury,
Benson, & Wallingford.

The Wharfingers and Proprietors of these Barges not accountable for any Damage by Fire or Water; for River Piracy, of small Parcels above the Value of Five Pounds, unless paid for accordingly; nor for Packages improperly packed, directed, marked, or described; or Leakage arising from bad Casks or Cooperage.

Randell, Howell & Randell, *Wharfingers, &c.*

It is particularly requested that the Gross Weight of all heavy Goods be specified in the Carman's Note.

34 Cases Mrs Palmer

Wharfage *landing &* Received by *J Cadd*
loading 8 " 6

Freight 1 " 14 " 0
£ 2 " 2 " 6   *23 Oct* 184*0*

☞ Please to send the Wharfage with your Goods.

TEW, Printer, 34, Queen-street, Cheapside, London.

Local spritsail barges still sailed up the Arun early in this century (above). Eighty years before, more primitive barges had reached Arundel. A series of canals built in the years after Waterloo attempted to create a through traffic between London & Portsmouth. But it was a short-lived venture; by the late forties the railway was already putting the canal barges out of business.

86

Chichester Harbour

The enclosed waters of Chichester harbour contain a number of quays, wharves and moorings known today by a multitude of weekend sailors. It is hardly surprising that these waters once sheltered numbers of small merchant vessels. Some were even built here; Foster of Emsworth was particularly well-known. His centreboard brigantine *Fortuna* (1892) represented a fresh approach to the design of coastal sail. This photograph was taken at Bosham in 1882 when T. Smart built the schooner *Two Sisters*, 115 tons. She was registered at Portsmouth. Kate Smart was the owner, for the Smarts as well as building and repairing vessels, owned and managed them. After being owned in Cornwall for many years the *Two Sisters* had disappeared from the *Mercantile Navy List* by 1938.

In this evocative photograph she is partially planked up. The ship up against the tiled cottage, the more pretentious dwelling with its barge-boarded gable, the ancient spire of Bosham church, the timber carriage to the right of the ship and the patent slip in the foreground are all so atmospheric that one can almost smell that foreshore.

The same atmosphere pervades this photograph taken at Bosham before World War I. It is compounded of the sagging tiles and the patched brickwork of the store, the timbers of the quay and the mud of channel. There are two local trading vessels—an apple-cheeked smack and a leeboard ketch barge discharging cargo into a waiting cart, two old men on the quay and the mist creeping in . . . The barge *Emerald*, 34 tons, built at Landport in 1877, was owned by J. J. Crampton of Landport in 1900. She is typical of the small boomie barges which traded to the ports between Poole, Chichester and the Isle of Wight. (Below)

The barquentine *Sarah Amy*, 158 tons, was one of the large vessels Foster built at Emsworth. She was launched in 1874 for Cox of Portsmouth (below).

Portsmouth Merchant Shipping

The story of the merchant sailing ships that served the creeks and wharves of Portsmouth and Langstone harbours deserves to be written up in depth. From the brigs and brigantines which brought coal and timber, to the smacks and barges which carried local agricultural produce, the total numbers involved would seem to have been extensive. The following four pictures from the Mortimer Collection in the National Maritime Museum simply skim the cream off the subject. The whole theme of Portsmouth's merchant shipping needs researching and recording.

The colliers, another grimy tribe of brigantines, discharged at the Camber. In the foreground is the *Albion*, 183 tons, built at Portsmouth in 1875 by J. T. Crampton who owned her himself.

Outward bound from Portsmouth harbour, possibly as early as the 1880s: sail drill is going on aboard the boys' training ship HMS *St Vincent*. In the foreground a standing topgallant schooner, having discharged a cargo somewhere at the back of Portsmouth harbour, is towing out to sea in a hurry. The foresail is set, the peak of the mainsail needs sweating up, and a hand is aloft loosing the lower topsail. The name of this attractive little schooner is partially hidden by the anchor, but on the original print the last four letters are visible, —*ldie*. I present this as a problem of ship identification!

A coal cargo has been discharged at the Camber and aboard this grimy old-timer the crew are washing down the decks. The amount of water on deck leads one to suppose that the lead scupper pipe is blocked. The man in the foreground has leaned his broom against the companionway, and he appears to be poking down the scupper hole with a thin rod. Poking down the narrow hole with a broom handle was usually frowned upon by a good mate for it was liable to fracture the lead, causing water to seep into the frames and the waterway. The author recalls being told off for doing this very thing.

Outward bound again! A small merchant brig tows out to sea behind an even smaller paddle-tug and against a naval, 'establishment' background. HMS *Victory* is at her moorings, over to the left is one of the naval training brigs, astern of the *Victory* is possibly an Admiralty yacht. A big Admiralty tug is on the gridiron. This picture could date back to the 1880s.

Southampton and the Solent

Southampton's latest maritime link with New York arrived on 11 August 1970. She was the full-rigged ship *Wavertree* and she was towed there all the way from Buenos Aires. The *Wavertree*, described by Mayor John Lindsay as 'the largest museum artifact brought to New York in one piece', was a steel full-rigged ship, 2118 tons, one of nine built by Oswald, Mordaunt & Co at Southampton, launched in 1885 for R. W. Leyland & Co of Liverpool. The *Wavertree*, in particular, was a noble example of a great Cape Horner of the late nineteenth century. T. L. Oswald came to Woolston from Sunderland in the 1870s, and began building first iron and later steel ships there. Many northcountry men came to Southampton to work for him. Early in this century his shipyard came under Messrs Thorneycroft.

Since she was dismasted off the Horn in 1910 the *Wavertree* had been a wool hulk at Punta Arenas, and a sand barge in Buenos Aires. Here she was discovered in 1966 and the South Street Seaport Museum of New York set out to save and restore her. This imaginative museum, with ambitious plans to bring to life a run-down section of the New York waterfront, obviously has a big job ahead to restore this great ship to her former pride, but a definite start has been made and prospects are bright. The *Wavertree* should become a permanent part of Southampton's maritime presence in New York.

Trade between the Isle of Wight and the mainland was the livelihood of a group of small ketches sailing out of Cowes and Newport. In 1865 Cowes owned twenty-three sailing vessels, mostly small fry of this type although there was one full-rigger, the ship *Levanter*, 868 tons. These Cowes ketches, built by Hansen at East Cowes or by White at West Cowes, were 25-30 tons, straight stemmed and square sterned. A characteristic of the rig was their immensely long main and mizzen gaffs nearly as long as their booms. The Cowes ketches had running bowsprits and long, light topmasts. The *Bee* (above) is exceptional in having a round stern. She was built by Hansen in 1801 and survived until 1926. Both she and the *Arrow* (right) were owned by Shepard Bros, a firm of Newport merchants. Hansen built the *Arrow*, 20 tons, in 1875. She was the last Cowes ketch trading and she survived until 1938.

Into the Edwardian elegance of pre-war Cowes sails the Russian schooner *Laima* of Windau in Latvia (now called Ventspils), where she was built in 1902. The product of some small peasant shipyard, everything about her is strong and heavy. With her deck cargo of Baltic timber and her trim workmanlike appearance, the *Laima* is a delightful contrast to the immaculate ship-rigged yacht in the background. She is the *Valhalla*, 1,211 tons, built at Leith in 1892 for Sir J. Laycock. Later owned by the Earl of Crawford, she was used by the French Government in the Dardanelles campaign. Soon after the war, when she was a French-owned merchant ship, she foundered off Cape St Vincent.

Shipwrecks and Disasters

As the Channel narrows towards its eastern end, the density of shipping upon it becomes greater. In the days of sail the losses were widespread; strandings, founderings, collisions and fire all took their toll. Probably the most spectacular stranding of a sailing ship was among the last. On 5 November 1910 the German five-masted ship *Preussen*, 5,081 tons, was in collision with the London Brighton & South Coast Railway's ss *Brighton* off Beachy Head. She was holed, her bowsprit broken and foremast weakened, and she drove up Channel, finally going ashore under the high cliffs in Crab Bay near the South Foreland. Her crew of forty-eight struggled for three sleepless nights; twelve tugs stood by and the Kaiser sent a telegram of sympathy. All in vain; the *Preussen* was a total loss.

The *Preussen*, which was the largest full-rigged sailing ship ever built, had been launched at Geestemunde in 1902 for F. Laeisz of Hamburg. She made twelve voyages altogether from Germany to the nitrate ports of the west coast of South America before being wrecked.

A much more typical shipwreck was that of the brig *Tally Ho*. She was a 189-ton collier built in 1854 by May at Shoreham; one of several owned by Thomas Gates & Co. She was wrecked near the Redoubt at Eastbourne on Boxing Day 1886. Captain Joseph Gasston, with his vessel making water badly in a SW gale, deliberately ran her ashore late in the evening. Fires were lit on the beach to assist the work of rescue. Those on shore could hear pathetic cries from the brig, 'Heave us a line; heave us a line!' Only three men caught the lines and got ashore. One man died after he got ashore; three perished in the breakers; one too numb and exhausted to catch a line, was swept off the wreck by the waves. Far too many of those elderly nineteenth-century wooden colliers were lost in similar fashion, all too often with a similar loss of life.

Possibly the most fearful maritime disaster ever to occur off south-east England was the loss of the ship *Northfleet*. She was outward bound to Tasmania with a cargo of railway iron, 350 labourers and a few wives and children. The *Northfleet* had left the Thames and anchored off Dungeness on the night of 22 January 1873. At 10.30 pm in clear weather she was rammed amidships by a steamer travelling at speed, which then made off. Within forty-five minutes the *Northfleet* had sunk; some 293 people were drowned.

This contemporary engraving, 'The Captain's Farewell', represents the scene as the *Northfleet's* longboat got away. There had been terrible panic among the passengers, and Captain Knowles had to stem a rush by firing his revolver. He saw his wife and the few other women into the boat with a number of labourers and three of the crew. Here he stands by the after davits, revolver in hand, waving to his wife in the forepart of the boat. The *Northfleet* went down a few minutes later. Captain Knowles and all his officers went down with her. Eighty-five people were saved, including those in the longboat.

The regular master of the *Northfleet* had been subpoenaed as a witness in the Tichborne trial and had been unable to take his ship to sea. His first officer, Mr Knowles, was offered the position with permission to take his twenty-four year old bride, whom he had married only a month before. In a century marked by so many terrible maritime tragedies the *Northfleet* sinking stands out as one of the most ghastly.

Mrs Knowles was awarded a Civil List pension in recognition of her husband's bravery. The guilty steamer was the Spanish *Murillo*, whose master escaped punishment by asserting that he had no idea that his ship had done any damage.

The *Dalhousie*, 800 tons, chartered by the White Horse Line of Australian passenger ships, left Blackwall for Sydney on 12 October 1853 with a crew of sixty, ten passengers and cargo worth £100,000. Her departure was reported from the Downs on 18 October. No more was heard of her until late the next afternoon when the brig *Mitchell Grove* (page 82) from Littlehampton anchored off Dover to report the loss of this magnificent ship. There was only one survivor, an AB named Joseph Reed.

At 4 am on 19 October under close-reefed topsails, in a strong SE gale and accompanied by a heavy sea, the *Dalhousie* had begun to roll deeply, going a long way over each time. At 5.30 she rolled right over on her starboard beam ends with her mastheads in the water. Within ten minutes the ship went under, Beachy Head light bearing NE by E 16 miles. Reed scrambled off the quarter gallery and kept afloat for about eleven hours until he was picked up by the *Mitchell Grove*.

On the night of 15 February 1859 the barque *Vizcaya* of Bilbao, bound from London to Bordeaux, was in collision with the Dutch ship *D'Elmira* off Beachy Head. The *Vizcaya's* crew clambered aboard the Dutchman leaving their own ship dismasted and badly damaged. Next morning the *Vizcaya* was sighted about four miles off Rottingdean. A tiny four-oared galley put off through the surf; the boatmen got aboard and anchored the barque. Before they set out they had sent to Newhaven asking for the first steamer that could get up steam to be sent to their help. Having done this the galley's crew firmly refused the assistance of some Brighton boats which had managed to reach the *Vizcaya*. The railway steamer *Lyons* put out from Newhaven, passed a hawser and by early afternoon had the barque safely inside the piers. The *Vizcaya* was later bought and re-rigged by J. Robinson of Littlehampton, and was finally lost on the Yorkshire coast in 1893. When brought into Newhaven the *Vizcaya* was armed with six guns. In 1939 one of these still survived—part of the foundation of a blacksmith's shop in Surrey St, Littlehampton.

In a SSW gale on the night of 27-8 December 1848 the Dutch East Indiaman *Twee Corn-elissen*, 750 tons, went aground in Pevensey Bay near No 55 Martello tower. She was a full-rigger, ninety-two days out of Batavia bound for Amsterdam. Lying-to for a pilot, she had become embayed and was driven ashore in heavy weather. At daybreak eighteen men got to the beach in their longboat, leaving the captain, mate and twelve men on board. At high water the Indiaman's decks were swept by great seas, forcing those on board to take to the mizzen rigging.

At 10.30 the Eastbourne lifeboat came down from windward and rounded-to round the Indiaman's stern. She took off thirteen men who slid down a rope from the cro'jack yard—the scene depicted in the engraving. Only when they were landed in a state of near-collapse was it realised that one man had been left on board. A telescopic survey of the wreck revealed a man lashed in the mizzen rigging. Four coastguards went out in a small boat, boarded the ship, cut the man free and brought him ashore, where he was pronounced to be dead. Two days later the wreck had completely broken up.

This wreck and rescue received wide press coverage. The *Illustrated London News* engraving, though lively enough, is less pleasing than Edwin Weedon's engravings which commenced a year or two later. The South Holland Society for the Preservation of Life from Shipwreck presented the coxswain of the Eastbourne lifeboat with its Gold Medal; the four coastguards were awarded bronze medals.

Like the *Preussen* the full-rigged ship *Polynesia*, 985 tons, which was built at Hamburg in 1874, was one of the splendid nitrate clippers of the Laeisz 'Flying P' line of Hamburg. In April 1890, on her way from Iquique to Antwerp with £30,000 worth of nitrate on board, she went ashore 300 yards east of Birling Gap near Beachy Head. A considerable amount of her cargo was unloaded and she was towed off; only to be beached, leaking badly, near the mouth of the Cuckmere. So badly damaged was the *Polynesia* that her wreck was sold by an Eastbourne firm of auctioneers. Her fittings and gear realised good prices, but the hull fetched only £125 for breaking up—an inglorious end for a noble ship.

In the misty morning of 7 March 1889 an oyster smack bound from Havre to Shoreham sighted a great sailing ship looming up ahead. She was the *Vandalia* of St John, New Brunswick. Only a dog was on board, and her bows were terribly damaged. Later that day the *Vandalia* ran ashore near Brighton's West Pier. Between Goring and Worthing 1,200 barrels of her cargo of petroleum washed ashore.

That morning at 1 o'clock she had been in head-on collision with a steamer twelve miles south of the Owers. One of the steamer's anchors fell on the *Vandalia* killing one of the sailors. Her crew then abandoned her. A steamer the *Duke of Buccleuch* of Barrow, known to have been in the vicinity with fifty-three men on board, was never seen again. She was supposed to have been the ship in collision with the *Vandalia*. The sailing ship remained on Brighton beach until 12 April, when she was refloated and towed to Shoreham for repair.

These pages may, perhaps, be a useful corrective to any tendency to view the great years of the sailing ship through a euphoric haze of romance. The sailing vessel was, in fact, a dangerous mode of conveyance! In narrow waters like the southeastern corner of England, it paid a ghastly price in lives and property.

The Arundel Shipmaster

As the great mass of nineteenth-century legislation relating to the Merchant Service began to take effect, merchant shipmasters and shipowners became involved in an ever increasing amount of paper work. Masters and owners of vessels sometimes had wooden boxes made like this one, to contain their ship's papers. Shipowners sometimes had a series of such boxes, one for each of the vessels in their fleet. In 1939 Banfield & Co, coal merchants of Brighton, still had in their office four such boxes belonging to their ships of fifty years before, the *Sarah*, the *Conflict*, the *Alice V. Goodhue* and the *Ebenezer*. Each box had a little painting of its ship on the front.

The brig *Sussex* of Shoreham was built at Kingston by May & Thwaites in 1840 for John Michell of Brighton. (Francis Cheeseman was her first master.) She was lost off Flamborough Head on 19 December 1875. John Michell was one of a large family originating from Rudgewick, the children of Edward and Mary Michell. A younger brother Matthew, their eleventh child and fourth son, was born at Steyning in 1824. From an early age he wished to join the Royal Navy. His mother who had strong leanings towards the Quakers, though not a member of the Society of Friends, prevented him from doing this. So he joined the merchant service in his early teens. It is now impossible to find out on which vessel he spent the early part of his career. The natural supposition that he spent some time at least upon his elder brother's ship is not borne out by the facts. Nowhere in the *Sussex's* crew lists does his name appear.

But on 15 November 1845, aged twenty-one, Matthew's name appears in the records as master of the schooner *Bertha* of Arundel, 126 tons. The *Bertha* was launched at Littlehampton by Thomas Isemonger, who owned 12 of her 64 shares. George Sparks of Littlehampton, merchant, owned 12. Matthew Michell of Steyning, master mariner, owned 8, George Michell of Steyning, brewer, owned 16, James Baker of Liverpool, who described himself as a shipowner, had 8, and Robert French of Littlehampton, solicitor, owned 8. Baker was the registered owner of the *Bertha* and presumably managed the ship's business.

Before his first voyage in his new ship Matthew Michell had his daguerreotype taken. He also had a painting done of the *Bertha* which is no longer in existence. (She would have looked something like the *Kingston* on page 64.) He commanded the *Bertha* for three years and in this time she made these voyages:

1845-6 Liverpool, Constantinople, Odessa, London
1846 London, Newcastle, Odessa, Limerick
1847 Liverpool, Constantinople, Limerick
1847-8 Limerick, Smyrna, London
1848 Liverpool, Beirut, Teignmouth
1848-9 Liverpool, Constantinople, Dublin

In Dublin Captain Michell was unfortunately attacked in a street brawl (this was a time of violence and unrest in Ireland) and was so seriously injured that he paid off from the *Bertha* in February 1849 and never went to sea again. The *Bertha* foundered in the North Atlantic in February 1852, homeward bound from Virginia. Matthew Michell retired to Southsea where he lived in a house with all the main windows facing the sea and a look-out —his 'Crow's Nest'—from which he could watch the passing shipping. He died about 1900, having lived through a period of the most fantastic maritime changes in history.

Acknowledgements

I am grateful to Edgar J. March for the information about the Cowes ketches on pages 96-7; to the City Librarians of Rochester, Portsmouth and Southampton for assistance; to the Curator of the Rye Museum and to the Curator of the Hastings Museum and Art Gallery; to Peter Stanford, President of the South Street Seaport Museum, New York, and to the Secretary of the Chicago Historical Society; to J. J. Hackett of Ramsgate for help with the interpretation of photographs; to A. G. W. Penney, Southwick, for help in tracing old pictures; to Frank Smith of Eastbourne for help over thirty years; and to G. A. Osbon of the photographic collection at the National Maritime Museum for the immense trouble he has taken in finding illustrations.

Sources of illustrations

The figures refer to the page numbers; the letters a or b indicate whether a picture is at the top or the bottom of a page. I have tried to give the original source of many of the illustrations from my own collection. With many of these very old photographs it is extremely difficult to trace from where they originated.

The two line drawings in the introduction were drawn by Adrian Small, master of the *Nonsuch* ketch, who is also responsible for the photograph on page 80.

Author's Collection, 1, 10, 11b, 13, 14, 24, 32, 38, 40, 42, 43b, 55, 57b, 63, 71, 74, 75, 78, 79a, 100, 105, 106. From *Illustrated London News*, 12, 16, 17, 21, 30, 101, 102, 103, 104, 112. Miss Pawson, 31. R. Hunt, 34 a and b. Miss Ginner, Hastings, 35, 36, 37, 39. Capt J. Robinson, Newhaven, 44a, 45, 46, 48, 49, 50, 51, 52, 53 a and b, 54 a and b, 56, 59, 61. H. Cheal, 58, 62 a and b (W. page photographer), 68. F. W. Spry, photographer, Littlehampton, 60, 83 a and b, 84. R. H. Penney & Sons, 70 a and b (P. Stabler, Sunderland, photographer), 76 (Alex Rambert, Port Louis, Ile Maurice, photographer). Capt John Short, 88.

Learned societies and public institutions—National Maritime Museum, 9, 18, 19, 43a, 57a, 85, 86, 87, 90, 91, 92, 93; the last four from the Mortimer Collection. Rye Museum, 20, 22, 23. Chicago Historical Society, 26, 27. Hastings Public Museum & Art Gallery, 28, 29. Sussex Archaeological Society, 41. Mayor and Corporation of Lewes, 44b. East Sussex County Record Office, 47. South Street Seaport Museum, New York, 94, 95. Alexander Turnbull Library, Wellington, NZ, 72 a and b, 73.

Commercial photographers etc—Sunbeam Photo, Margate, 14, 15, 81. Manning Galleries, 71 New Bond St, W1, 33. Beken & Sons, Cowes, 96, 97, 98. *Country Life*, 99.

Private persons—T. A. Bagley, 2. R. J. Passey, 11a. John Bowen 25 a and b. A member of the family which owned the *Kingston*, 64 a and b. H. O. Hill, 65, 82. A. G. W. Penney, 66, 67. Cecil M. Ayling, 69. Alec Hurst, 77. Jack Neale, 79b. Margaret Michell, 107. Mary W. Bouquet, 108.

Suggestions for Further Reading

Henry Brett—*White Wings*, Auckland, NZ 1924. Valuable for its information about the Penney ships in the New Zealand emigrant trade.

Frank C. Bowen—*London Ship Types*, London 1938. Information about the *Alastor* and about the Watkins' tugs.

F. G. G. Carr—*Sailing Barges*, London 1951.

Henry Cheal—*Ships and Mariners of Shoreham*, London 1909. A pioneer port study particularly useful for nineteenth-century material.

W. Clark Russell—*Betwixt the Forelands*, London c 1890.

Clayton's Annual Register of Shipping and Port Charges, London and Hull 1865.

George Keate—*Sketches from Nature, taken and coloured in a Journey to Margate*, 5th edition, London 1802. Written about 1780 this was a best-seller in its day. It gives a most amusing account of life aboard a Margate hoy.

G. S. Laird Clowes—*British Fishing and Coastal Craft*, HMSO 1937.

A Maritime Exhibition, Catalogue of an Exhibition held at Michelham Priory, 1963. Most useful for source material on Sussex maritime history.

My own *No Gallant Ship*, London 1959, may still be of use. I have used material from the nineteenth-century files of the *Sussex Express*, the *Illustrated London News*, the *Chicago Magazine* and the *Chicago Press*. My own articles in the now defunct *Sussex County Magazine* between 1936 and 1939 contain a good deal more detailed material than space allows for in this book. The pre-war *Sea Breezes* in the 30s contain detailed fleet lists for the Bull and Penney ships. The files of the *Mariner's Mirror*, *Sea Breezes* and *Ships and Ship Models* may all be consulted with advantage.